How Annuities & Life Insurance
Can Help You Live

YOUR LIFE

YOUR WAY

Published by CelebrityPress®, Orlando, FL

CelebrityPress® is a registered trademark.

Printed in the United States of America.

ISBN: 978-0-9961978-2-3
LCCN: 2015937404

This publication is designed to provide accurate and authoritative information with regard to the subject matter covered. It is sold with the understanding that the publisher is not engaged in rendering legal, accounting, or other professional advice. If legal advice or other expert assistance is required, the services of a competent professional should be sought. The opinions expressed by the authors in this book are not endorsed by CelebrityPress®, and are the sole responsibility of the author rendering the opinion.

CelebrityPress®
520 N. Orlando Ave, #2
Winter Park, FL 32789
or call 1.877.261.4930

Visit us online at: www.CelebrityPressPublishing.com

How Annuities & Life Insurance Can Help You Live

YOUR LIFE

YOUR WAY

By

Greg Parady

In Dedication

To my wife, Jenni – for supporting me and allowing me the freedom to pursue my dreams. . . even if it means working 30 hours a day.

To my son, Bennett – for the daily reminder of what's important in life and the nightly reminders of how much I have taken a good night of sleep for granted all these years.

To my 2nd grade teacher, Jean Bennett – a special thanks to you and Gene for supporting and encouraging me for the past 35 years.

I want to acknowledge my partner and friend, Cindy Nazzaro, for helping me realize my vision for our company—and redefining the definition of world class service.

And, to all of my clients – thank you for your ongoing trust, support and business. Without you, this book would not be a reality and my company would not have achieved the success we have enjoyed.

TABLE OF CONTENTS

DISCLAIMERS

The following is for informational purposes only on issues that many people consider in making the decision as to whether or not they should buy insurance products, including annuities.

- *This information is not designed to be a recommendation to buy any specific financial product or service.*

- *Pursuant to IRS Circular 230, it is not intended to provide any specific tax or legal advice and cannot be used to avoid tax penalties or to promote, market or recommend any tax plan or arrangement. Please note that Greg Parady does not give legal or tax advice. We encourage you to speak with a qualified tax advisor or attorney.*

- *Social security election is an important decision. We have both a CFP and a CPA on our team who can help guide people through the complexities of this decision. Parady Financial is not in any way affiliated with the Social Security Administration.*

Parady Financial Group, Inc. works closely with Parady Tax Solutions, LLC and Parady Investments, LLC to provide various services to our clients. The Parady Annuity and Life Insurance division of Parady Financial Group provides retirement income planning strategies and sells fixed indexed annuities and life insurance products. Parady Tax Solutions is an accounting and tax firm that helps provide tax planning and tax preparation for our Parady Financial Group clients. Parady Investments is a Registered Investment Advisory offering financial planning services; not all Parady employees are securities registered, including Greg Parady. A full list of Parady team members and their licenses and certifications is available online at: http://www.paradyfinancial.com/parady-financial-staff-licenses-certifications/.

Notes on Annuities
*Annuity guarantees are backed by the financial strength and claims-paying ability of the issuing carrier.
**Some annuities may have a lifetime income guarantee as part of the base policy; others may have riders available for additional premium that provide this benefit.
Compliance Review: FCA #1500024-R

FOREWORD

BY ED SLOTT,
CPA AND RETIREMENT EXPERT

Named "The Best Source for IRA Advice" by *The Wall Street Journal*
and called "America's IRA Expert" by *Mutual Funds Magazine*
www.irahelp.com

Parady Financial Group has your retirement strategy.

If someone told you that they could guarantee that you won't ever lose money in retirement, you would rightly doubt that claim, or say "Where can I sign up for that?" Greg Parady, a unique individual has built a well-respected retirement planning and tax-planning firm, Parady Financial Group, focused on that core principal – guaranteed retirement income, and his clients love it.

But that's only the financial side of what Greg and his team are about. Even more impressive are the wonderful relationships Parady Financial Group has built with their clients. This is not a blind endorsement. I have seen this first hand. When I visit with their clients, it seems like I am at family function, with food, music, entertainment and oh yes, great retirement planning information. When was the last time you danced at a financial planning seminar?

Their clients are like his family and it shows. It is so nice to see retired people so happy and worry free, knowing they have reliable supplemental income during their retirement years. Parady Financial Group has cultivated these relationships over many years by creating customized financial plans based only on what's best for their clients and their families. You can see that his clients are not worried about outliving their money – the number one fear in America's retirees today. That's why they are so lively and happy, and it's fun to be around them. They make me feel young! You really have to see this for yourself, like I have.

But there's more. Another ingredient that makes this all work so well for Parady Financial is education. They never stop educating themselves. Clients need to know that their financial and insurance professionals have the specialized knowledge of how to leverage their retirement assets to make it last.

Financial and insurance professionals generally help you accumulate money, but that's only half of the game. Accumulating money is great, but protecting your assets and making them last is often the missing ingredient in most retirement plans. At Parady, Greg created a strategic planning firm that focuses on two of the biggest financial challenges in retirement: protection of assets and minimization of taxes.

In retirement, it's what you keep after taxes that counts, because that's the money you can actually spend and enjoy. More taxes means less for you, just when you need it most – in retirement.

I believe taxes are the single biggest factor that separates people from their retirement dreams and money. But the problem is that most firms do not have the specialized tax planning knowledge, and that puts their clients' retirement savings in jeopardy.

Parady Financial Group make it a priority to help you minimize taxes in retirement. I know that for a fact because I see Greg and the Parady team of professionals at our advanced training programs on retirement tax planning as members of "Ed Slott's Master Elite IRA Advisor Group." Less than one percent of professionals in the country have this level of training. If you are heading into retirement or already there, wouldn't you want to be working with a firm that values both education and client relationships above all else? Of course you would.

Greg and Parady Financial Group's story is a model for all others. When I see their clients, I know you want your trusted financial and insurance professionals to operate like this. Don't you?

- Ed Slott, CPA
Retirement Expert and Founder of
Ed Slott's Elite IRA Advisor Group
www.irahelp.com

INTRODUCTION

Retirement is a lot like climbing a mountain.

I know this may not be the first comparison that pops into your mind. But then again, helping people retire with greater financial confidence is my business, so if *anyone* is going to make that comparison, I guess it should probably be me. However, it's also an analogy that makes a lot of sense, especially since my experience climbing to the summit of Longs Peak in Colorado with my little brother, Luke.

My brother had been a world-class rock climber since he was a teenager. Me...well, I'd at least *seen* a rock. I prided myself on staying in good shape, but I still knew that if I was going to keep up with Luke on a seven-and–a-half mile trek to the summit of a 14,000-foot mountaintop, I was going to need a little bit of preparation.

Preparation is important to retirement – if you picked up on that, great job. However, we're not even close to the important part of the story. That comes later.

Once I committed to the climb, I got serious about preparation. I refused to be shown up by my younger sibling. So, I spent six intense months training for the hike. I ate all the right foods, jogged several miles a day, and hit the gym to train on the treadmill as often as possible.

The treadmill was the most crucial aspect of my regimen. Why? I live in Florida, a state that is notoriously beautiful, but also notoriously flat. The only way I could get ready for the steep incline that Longs Peak no doubt had in store for me was to simulate it on a machine. So I did. I worked my way up, higher and higher through all the machine settings until I maxed out the treadmill at a 45-degree angle. I thought that should prepare me to climb a mountain!

It was my daily routine for months.

Next, since I live at sea level, I knew I would need to acclimate my body to the thin air and high altitude of the Rocky Mountains. So I arrived in Colorado a full month before we were scheduled to climb to get my body used to functioning at a higher altitude. I fully enjoyed the experience, learning how to fly fish in the rivers and streams of Estes Park while my body gradually adjusted.

When the day of the climb arrived, I certainly felt ready. Luke had planned our departure for midnight, which seemed a little crazy, but he was the expert. We set out in the dark of night loaded down with headlamps, backpacks stuffed with water and hydration gels, multiple layers of clothing and rain gear. You name it, we brought it.

At first, all those months of training seemed to serve me well. However, I still wasn't prepared for the way the altitude affected me. We had to stop so often to drink water and just catch our breath that we averaged less than one mile per hour. Having always taken pride in my health and athleticism, I found this a little humbling.

But at 5:30 a.m. I got my (first) reward. After five and a half hours of walking, stumbling and resting in the dark, I witnessed the most beautiful sunrise I had ever seen. The sun actually rose below us! It was one of the most amazing and breathtaking experiences of my life.

Four and a half hours later, after nine hours of climbing, I had an even more amazing experience. We reached the summit.

Words cannot describe how beautiful it was, standing on top of the world under a cloudless sky. Even more indescribable was the tremendous feeling of personal achievement that flooded me from my head to my toes. I could have stayed there for hours, basking in the beauty and the joy of what was definitely the greatest physical accomplishment of my life.

And I wasn't alone in my exultation. At least 100 other hikers were up there with us, each reveling in their own success upon reaching the summit. And some of them were really making a day of it. They were sitting on rocks chatting, taking pictures – some were even eating lunch.

My brother and I? Not so much. Almost the minute we reached the summit, Luke was already talking about our descent. My self-congratulatory basking and photo-snapping lasted just 12 minutes. We climbed for nine hours and all I got was 12 lousy minutes?

Now, truth be told, since Luke is my little brother, I don't always listen to him. But he was absolutely adamant that we begin our descent immediately. And, just in case I was thinking about putting up a fight, he actually started climbing down before I had a moment to question his decision. He took off at breakneck speed, which indicated to me that, whatever the reason, he was basically on a mission to get back down. Maybe he left his wallet back at the bottom?

There wasn't much I could do except take off after him and try to keep up. And that's when it hit me. In all those months of training and preparation, I never once put the treadmill on a DECLINE setting.

Day after day, week after week, month after month, I concentrated solely on climbing UP the mountain. It was all about getting to the top. In my excitement and inexperience, I forgot an important rule of physics: what goes up, must come down. And now, what was coming down…was me!

It never crossed my mind that I might need to train different muscles to navigate the descent part of our adventure. If I had, I would have learned that, believe it or not, climbing down a steep mountain can be even more challenging than climbing up.

My body let me know pretty quickly. I wound up trailing behind Luke, first by five minutes, then ten minutes, for what seemed like forever. Luckily, at around 12,000 feet, Luke finally stopped for a drink and an energy bar, giving me the time I needed to catch up. I stood there, sucking air as hard as I could, until I was finally able to form the words to say something amounting to: "Why did you take off so fast???" In response, he told me a story I will never forget. And, yes, it's this part of the story that really, really relates to retirement.

Luke's Story
"I was on this mountain two years ago and was about 200 feet from the top when we were caught in a sudden lightning and hail storm. I wasn't on this trail though. I was totally exposed on the mountain face climbing with some friends.

(My brother is a rock climber, not a hiker. He does the crazy stuff.)

"The lightning came out of nowhere around noon and was cracking and thundering all around us. I thought it was all over. As with most climbs, I set a goal to reach the peak and that day was no different. I didn't know then that the peak of this summit is like a magnet for electricity, so when it warms up around noon there is often a thunderstorm that is attracted to the same spot almost daily.

(Sure enough, as he spoke, I saw huge black clouds enveloping the summit we had enjoyed just minutes earlier. No wonder he was in such a hurry to get down the mountain!)

"The success of this trip, or any trip, isn't measured by reaching the top; success is measured by how well you navigate the

challenges facing you once you've reached the top. The people that are up there right now are in danger, and they're making decisions under extreme stress. They're tired and weak from the climb, and they're all panicking to get down from there. It's never a good idea to make big decisions under extreme duress.

It is completing the trip that tells whether you've achieved your goal. You must be prepared for the downhill before you begin the uphill climb. And you must be prepared for it prior to the ascent. We began this trip at midnight so that we could reach the top early enough to get out of harm's way prior to the storms."

It is the exit strategy that determines achievement. Who could have known that the single biggest reason that our trip was successful was the starting time? Only someone who had been there before would know the risks and plan appropriately to mitigate them. I hoped all those people we left behind with their cameras and their sandwiches were okay.

I learned a lot about my brother that day. I learned a lot about myself too. But the greatest lesson I took away from Longs Peak was about life – and, yes, about how the way most of us live our lives pertains to my career and my passion working with retirement strategies.

Because when it comes to retirement, most people are a lot like I was. I thought I did everything I needed to do to prepare to climb Longs Peak. Just like those soon-to-be retirees who plan, sacrifice, save, invest, and utilize whatever resources they can to help them get to the top of the retirement mountain. That's their goal, just like reaching the top of Longs Peak was my goal. They have no idea that, in reality, this is really only half of the planning.

They don't always know about which storms could arise, or about the potential dangers or obstacles that they could face once they have reached the top of that peak. Once they are actually "in retirement" that doesn't mean the journey is over.

In reality, reaching the top of Retirement Mountain is only the first half of the journey. Once they make it to the summit, retirees may be just like the people eating sandwiches on top of Longs Peak. They need an exit strategy, or a plan for how they're going to navigate down the mountain, so they can be prepared for possible challenges and better enjoy the benefits of their hard work. That's what this book is all about.

CHAPTER 1

WHO AM I…AND WHY DID I WRITE THIS BOOK?

I think the concept of greater financial confidence has always resonated with me because I had what a lot of people would consider a traumatic childhood. I was the oldest of five kids, and when I was 12, my normally healthy stepfather suffered his first heart attack. He was a dentist with a small practice in Harrison, Maine. But once he had that heart attack, he couldn't work. As the oldest, I had to grow up quickly and help take responsibility for my siblings, including my ten-year-old sister, three-year-old brother and twin one-year-old baby sisters.

I remember experiencing a lot of fear and anxiety, wondering if my stepfather would ultimately be okay, and/or if our family would survive financially. Luckily, after a few months, my stepfather was able to return to work, and life returned to normal… for a while. A few years later, he had a second heart attack. And since I was now a teenager, everything felt like it was on my shoulders. I worried about my family, my Dad's health, and how the next bill would be paid. The pressure took a toll on me, both academically and socially. Suddenly, I didn't feel like I had much in common with the other kids. I felt disconnected.

Once I was out of high school, I didn't have the luxury of being able to afford to go to college. However, my childhood experiences did leave me with a built-in survival instinct, a strong work ethic, and an intense desire to succeed. I was also an outgoing person, so retail seemed like a good place to start my career. I went to work for a division of the Macy's department stores in Boston, MA, and it turned out to be a good choice – I was promoted several times, rising from a "guy on the floor" to supervisory positions. I felt like I was on the path to a career in management.

Then my father had his third heart attack, and I moved back to Maine to help the family again. I needed to find work in my home-town. But without a college degree, I was turned down for some good sales positions. However, thanks to my retail experience at Macy's, I was finally able to get a job in retail management with a local sporting goods store. Unfortunately, working in a local retail store doesn't pay a lot of money, and there wasn't a huge opportunity for growth.

So I kept my eyes open for a better opportunity if one presented itself. That's when I met the guys at Bankers Life and Casualty. There I began what is still my career today, selling insurance designed to help protect families – families like mine – from the same kinds of financial stresses that I faced as a boy.

At only 22 years old, the people at Bankers Life and Casualty took a chance on me. After all, I was completely new to the field, and I didn't have a college degree. So, during my interview, they suggested I start by "shadow riding" a guy named John to get the hang of things.

I learned a lot from John. But I didn't exactly learn what people expected. I went on four sales appointments with John, and they did not go well. His prospective clients wanted help – they tried to tell us about their specific concerns and health issues and goals. Yet all John seemed to care about was selling them a one-size-fits-all product. These people wanted solutions, but all John wanted was to make a sale and get his commission – and this fact was painfully obvious to anyone that was sitting next to him.

At some point during the day, I asked John how much money he made in the last year, and he told me he had made $40,000 in the past eight months. That was enough for me. I figured if John could make $40K in eight months without even listening to people, that if I focused on *helping* people, listening to them and working with them to find the strategies they needed, I would make even more. I called my manager and told him that I was ready to join the company and start a new career.

And things worked out great for me. I was named "Rookie Agent of the Month" in my first month. In my second, I broke the company's sales record. It was all pretty exciting.

Before long, as a long-term care insurance, annuities and life insurance agent with Bankers Life and Casualty, I became one of the youngest people to ever qualify for the Million Dollar Roundtable.*** I was also the youngest member on the company's Executive Council.

When I became part of a big company like Bankers Life, I was considered a "captive agent" which simply means that I was only able to offer Bankers Life products. While they offered many competitive products, not all of them were suitable for my clients' needs. I wasn't able to offer what I believed to be the most competitive strategies in each individual client situation. This clashed with what I saw as my primary mission – to work directly with people to provide customized strategies for their individual retirement needs.

When I founded Parady Financial in 2001, I decided our focus would be customization. I offered a wider range of quality products and choices than I was able to offer at Bankers, and worked with my clients to help create customized retirement strategies designed to meet their specific needs and goals.

*** Founded in 1927, the Million Dollar Round Table (MDRT), The Premier Association of Financial Professionals®, is a global, independent association of the world's leading life insurance and financial services professionals. MDRT members demonstrate exceptional professional knowledge, strict ethical conduct and outstanding client service. MDRT membership is recognized internationally as the standard of excellence in the life insurance and financial services business. More information can be found at www.mdrt.org.

As we grew, I also strove to build a knowledgeable staff with a diverse range of skills. Today, that team includes several highly-educated Certified Public Accountants (CPAs) and Certified Financial Planners (CFPs), Certified Annuity Specialists (CASs) and many licensed insurance agents. Together, we combine our unique abilities and passion to help make amazing things happen for our clients.

What's my unique ability and passion? Surrounding myself with a team of professionals, dedicated to helping people realize the retirement dreams they envisioned as they were climbing the mountain – and, in the remainder of this book, my goal is to share some ideas that may help make amazing things happen for you.

CHAPTER 2

THE CHANGING RETIREMENT LANDSCAPE

Retirement has changed a lot since our parents (mostly our fathers, back then) picked up their last paychecks and their gold watches and settled in for what they could confidently believe would be a life of well-earned rest and relaxation.

There were a lot of tools helping keep those golden years golden. For example, if you retired in 1975 or even 1985, chances were good that you would be retiring with a solid, reliable pension.

Back then, most people worked for one or two companies for the entire span of their career. There was little reason not to be loyal because successful companies offered their employees incentives to remain with their company for decades. One of the biggest and most significant perks of that era was the pension plan – also known as the "defined benefit plan." When you retired, your employer would continue to send you regular payments, predetermined by a formula based on your earnings history, years of service and age. While lower than your salary when you retired, it would guarantee a decent income for the rest of your life. These pension plans were paid for by the employer and were considered the "reward" for years of loyalty. They were very common in the trades, government and corporate world.

29

Of course, many people today are still retiring with pensions. However, pensions on their own don't guarantee financial confidence – they need to be properly funded and well managed in order to support the benefits being promised. We'll discuss pension plans in more detail later on.

Then there's healthcare. You're no doubt aware that healthcare costs have risen exponentially since 1975. Plus, back then, many companies also offered and paid health insurance benefits that lasted for the rest of their employees' lives too. Today?

Well, now there's Medicare.

And those generous company benefit packages are only one aspect of the retirement landscape that has changed in recent years.

The generation that retired in 1975 grew up during the Great Depression. After the crash of 1929, a lot of U.S. workers weren't interested in the stock market. Even though back in the 70s there wasn't the same level of stock-market volatility we've seen over the past two decades, many conservative-minded people weren't comfortable dealing with the uncertainty of the market. They wanted predictable and reliable financial strategies. But that was okay. Because back in the 70s, you could still earn a steady, predictable income simply by putting your money in the bank.

Remember when banks used to give away toasters as an incentive to put your money there? In my experience, today most banks don't even pay enough interest to *buy* a toaster. In fact, some banks charge more in fees than they pay in interest!

But back then, one of the best options for many was actually putting money in the bank. Banks were considered reliable, and they paid interest – so much interest you might even have been able to live off of it.

So let's look back at the whole picture. The 1975-era retiree likely had a decent company pension (or two), received health benefits, and had a bank savings account that paid interest.

Today's retirement, however, is highly unlikely to follow a similar scenario.

Many of today's retirees simply don't have access to the same tools or financial benefits their parents enjoyed. At the same time, most of the people retiring today are going to live much longer lives than their parents did. Since most of them don't have a retirement package that includes anything like a corporate pension or health insurance benefits paid by the company, they'll have to rely on IRAs or 401(k)s and other financial vehicles to help provide enough retirement income to support their lifestyles. With today's employer-sponsored plans, the responsibility of managing your financial vehicles is in the hands of the individual employee.

Which is an awful lot of pressure to put on an employee's retirement funding.

Of course, there's the stock market. As I'm writing these words, the stock market is at another all-time high. But who would be surprised if we had another major correction – or even a stock market crash – in the next few years? Or even months or weeks? Market volatility is normal now, and because we are now in a global economy, the velocity of this volatility can impact even conservative investors. I call it the "Economic Snow Globe" – seems like every time the snow settles down, someone or something comes along and shakes it back up again.

Luckily, there is some good news. If you're retiring today, there's a good chance you have some assets socked away. You've probably spent the last four decades or so living a lifestyle built around the support and benefits provided by the company or companies you worked for – and hopefully you've gotten good advice on what benefits and financial strategies are best for your needs during your accumulation years to allow you to build a retirement nest-egg.

When you walk out that door from work for the last time, you'll be expected to successfully figure out how to handle your retirement assets all on your own. For the very first time in your life, you will have to figure out how to *take* money out of your assets every month instead of how much to put in to your retirement funds.

The good news: you have access to all this money. The bad news: few benefits. Plus you're faced with the overwhelming task of making those assets – your retirement funds – behave like or provide all the benefits you had at work.

It's no wonder so many of today's retirees struggle to understand the ins and outs of retirement income planning. For 30 years or more you've planned and saved for retirement under an umbrella of options. Now, things have flipped and you will need to start doing the exact opposite.

If you're like most of today's retirees, that's a tall order for you to handle on your own. You should find a team of trusted financial professionals that will provide reliable advice to help protect, preserve and enhance your retirement lifestyle.

Your generation of retirees is different, too. Add the additional stress of learning how to cope with or how to care for:

- An aging parent – including making health, financial and living decisions for that parent.
- Adult children – many who have been affected by this last recession and have been leaning on Mom and Dad to help out.
- Grandchildren – who you certainly want to enjoy, and may also want to provide certain things for.

No wonder they call Baby Boomers the "Sandwich Generation." In light of these new realities, maybe they should call them the "Triple Decker Sandwich Generation!"

However, there are some reliable, proven retirement income planning strategies that can help provide you with the income you need to be sure your retirement goals are met.

CHAPTER 3

RETIREMENT MOUNTAIN

Because we no longer live in an era where we can count solely on our former employers to provide a significant portion of our retirement income, many of us have had to take on that role ourselves. And many of us have dedicated ourselves to making and accumulating money for our retirement with a passion.

As a group, we're very industrious. We work and save and invest for years, with the goal to climb as high as we can on "Retirement Mountain." After all, the higher we can climb now, the better off we will be later on down the road, right?

This is the *accumulation phase*, or as I like to call this – the first phase of the Retirement Mountain journey.

Frequently, the accumulation phase is the only phase a lot of people are concerned about or put any thought into. Just like when I was training to climb Longs Peak, a lot of folks believe that once they reach the summit they will be able to enjoy the view, and everything else will take care of itself.

But, as I learned on that mountaintop in Colorado, once you've reached the top, you're only halfway there. It's equally important to strategize on the best route for you to follow on the way down.

The next phase is the *distribution phase* of life, and it's just as important as the accumulation phase. Maybe even more important.

Why? Once you stop working, mistakes and risks can have a bigger impact on your future because you're no longer getting steady, regular paychecks from your company. Also it can be a lot harder to earn back any losses you may have in the market, simply because there isn't enough time to recover. Look at it this way – if you trip at the bottom of the mountain, when you're just starting to climb up, you probably won't fall very far; you can stand up, dust yourself off and continue climbing. But a fall once you are near or have reached the top could mean you fall further and it could be harder to recover.

Reaching the top of Retirement Mountain is a major transition point in most people's lives. It's the point where they make the shift from the accumulation phase – when they were climbing the mountain – to the distribution phase on the trip back down.

I know this transition well. I like working with people that are nearing or have already reached the summit of Retirement Mountain, helping them navigate through the specific financial challenges that retirees can face. Since 1996, I have worked with more than 2,000 families, successfully designing retirement strategies that use annuities and other insurance products, allowing them to feel more financially confident during the distribution phase of their retirement while enjoying their assets and meeting their retirement needs and goals.

I think of each of these strategies as an "exit strategy" – the same kind of exit strategy my brother used to get us down Longs Peak safely. Your exit strategy should be customized to fit your goals, in order to take you from where you are today – on top of the mountain – to where you want to be tomorrow.

The bottom line is, there's often a big difference between the process of accumulating wealth during your working years, and utilizing and enjoying those assets in your retirement years. It takes different financial "muscles" and a different mindset. Fortunately, with the proper use of annuities and other insurance products, there are many conservative strategies you can employ that can help you enjoy your assets, and meet your retirement needs and goals.

Most people started their careers at the bottom and worked their way up. They've been through college and/or the military, marriage, sometimes divorce, kids, their kids' marriages, their kids' divorces, changing jobs...but through it all they've stayed focused on making money and putting away retirement funds.

Many of them – maybe you – worked for a company (or companies) that provided a wide range of benefits that included various types of insurance (life, health, dental, vision, disability) as well as a retirement income plan (401(k) or IRA).

Most importantly, they made the climb up Retirement Mountain easier. Your seed money came out of your paychecks before you even saw it. And perhaps your company even matched a portion of the funds for your retirement strategy!

But you had things that, as you reach the summit of Retirement Mountain, you'll soon be leaving behind – like paychecks! Routinely, you received a paycheck. Over time, those paychecks probably got bigger and bigger. You counted on the reliability of those checks, and you probably learned how to manage money on a monthly or bi-weekly basis.

Of course you had time: Plenty of time to learn, to make mistakes, to correct those mistakes, to experience change and to allow your funds and seed money to take root and grow.

All in all, your career most likely provided you with a sense of more financial confidence, allowing you a measure of freedom knowing you had a retirement income strategy for your future needs.

But when you retire, things change. Your accumulation strategy may no longer be applicable – after all, you were accumulating FOR retirement. Many of you reading this are very near or already retired!

Most of my clients have been accumulating for years, planning for their future, raising their families, and frequently putting the needs of others before their own for decades – all so that they can enjoy the retirement they've dreamed of.

But as they near the top of Retirement Mountain, they begin to face new challenges. What they do with their money as they reach the top may be some of the most important financial decisions of their lives. They face several challenges that their parents and earlier generations may not have had to deal with. These include:

- Fewer employer-sponsored retirement benefits, such as pensions and health insurance coverage.

- Market fluctuations that have become more prevalent, making retirement income planning difficult to predict or rely on.

- Some of the lowest interest rates of the past forty years.[1]

- Healthcare costs rising at unpredictable rates.[2]

- The very real possibility of living 30 years or more in retirement.

This last point is a concern for many Baby Boomers and current retirees. What if they outlive their money? With corporate pensions going the way of the dinosaur, how can they guarantee they have enough income for life?

Because of these questions, most retirees are probably conservative when it comes to spending retirement assets. They want to protect what they've worked so hard to accumulate, and they come to us seeking what I consider to be smarter ways to help protect those assets now that they've already accumulated "enough" to retire.

Over the years, a lot of my clients have shared with me that their ultimate goal is not to build a giant group of assets that will be passed on to their beneficiaries. They want to enjoy what they've worked for – and they want it to last as long as they do. Of course, they want to leave the kids or grandkids money when they're gone and they still want reasonable returns.

They come to us looking for a retirement income strategy that is built around their unique goals and concerns, not a one-size-fits-all product. They want to work with a team who will help them design a personal strategy to fit their specific needs. A strategy that can take a portion of those retirement assets they accumulated on the way up the mountain and use them to help enjoy the distribution phase for as long as they live.

I'll spotlight some of the most common challenges of protecting your assets and creating income once you reach the top of Retirement Mountain. I'll also share my personal opinion on what I believe are some viable options to help provide greater financial confidence for people who are entering, or are already in, retirement. People I work with are seeking guarantees for a portion of their retirement income. They want to spend more time enjoying life and less time concerned about how market risk may impact their income. They want protection from the "Economic Snow Globe."

Because if we are talking about guaranteeing income or principal while in or nearing retirement, then we are talking about annuities – and annuities are what Parady Financial uses to help provide our clients with predictable guaranteed* income strategies for life.**

CHAPTER 4

WHAT ARE ANNUITIES?

Chances are you haven't heard much about annuities, because, to be honest, they're not very flashy. They are insurance contracts, so most product types are not exposed to market fluctuations. Most product types are not designed to compete with the stock market, so they may seem kind of boring.

However, when used properly, *annuities can help pay you income every single month for the rest of your life.*[**] How flashy do you need your retirement funds to be anyway?

But, because there are different types of annuities that require specific understanding, they are often not fully or properly discussed in financial news outlets. Pick up a retirement magazine and the focus is unlikely to be on annuities. They are more likely to talk about picking great funds or stocks to retire at 50 and often try to entice you with pictures of yachts and exotic private beaches. Which is all nice, but most of us live in the real world.

If you have a modest retirement nest egg, and are simply trying to generate a steady predictable income stream that you're guaranteed not to outlive, hedge for inflation, and protect against the downside of the market, annuities could be an important part of your overall financial plan.

They may not be flashy in terms of growth or accumulation. But when it comes to creating guaranteed income, annuities just *work*.

An annuity is a contract with an insurance company. In exchange for premium(s), the issuing company will make payments to you on a future date or series of dates. The amount of the payment is determined by a variety of factors, including the amount of premium(s) you paid, your age when you begin annuity payments, and possibly your gender. They can be specifically designed to guarantee* income, and when they are used for that purpose, they can be powerful retirement planning tools.

There are different types of annuities, and many different benefit options. Annuities have different limitations and features, which may vary by carrier, product or state. Also, annuity riders may be available for an annual premium to provide additional benefits or income guarantees. Your financial professional can help you understand the various types and options that are available for your needs.

Annuities can either be immediate, which means they can begin distributing payments soon after you buy it, or deferred, which means the annuity payments are deferred until a later date.

The annuity payments from immediate or deferred annuities can be guaranteed* for a specific period of time, or for the rest of your life.** There can also be other payout options available, such as joint life annuities to continue covering a spouse, should one of the married couple die.

A common type of deferred annuity is a "fixed annuity." These annuities guarantee your principal will earn a minimum interest rate, which is set by the carrier. They may be able to earn a higher interest rate, but only the minimum is guaranteed.

Any interest your contract earns is tax-deferred, which means you won't be taxed on the interest until it is withdrawn. Distributions from annuities are taxed as ordinary income, and, if taken prior to age 59½, may be subject to a 10% federal tax penalty.

Because annuities are designed to distribute steady income payments, annuities can provide valuable benefits for today's pre-retirees and retirees. If one of your retirement concerns is "outliving" your money, annuities should be considered for part of your strategy.

With a fixed index annuity, a low interest is guaranteed,* and the potential for additional interest is tied to an external index in the market. If the index does well, your annuity is credited with more interest. If the index turns down, your principal and any gains you have made in interest are protected from loss. Fixed Index Annuities can be an important part of your overall retirement strategy when trying to generate a steady predictable income stream that you're guaranteed* not to outlive,** which helps to protect against inflation, and protects against the downside of the market.

Another type of annuity is a variable annuity. Variable annuities rely on the underlying performance of the stock market and investment choices within the contract. They may see gains or experience losses depending on positive or negative market fluctuations. We do not sell variable annuities.

Fixed index annuities are designed to handle the challenges facing today's retirees, especially people that want to minimize or eliminate exposure to the stock market fluctuations.

My opinions are based on experience. I've been working with retirees since the age of 22 and began my career in 1996. I have only used fixed and fixed index annuities. They may be controversial at times, and many "experts" have opinions about their value. However, I'm not the only person who believes in the power of these annuities. Wharton professor, David Babbel, conducted the Babbel Fixed Index Annuity study (last updated January 6, 2011). He was asked by *Annuity Digest* to summarize the results. His response captures the essence of the 98-page report in a relatively brief statement:

"The genesis of the study is as follows. There has been a lot of misinformation in the popular press regarding FIAs [Fixed Indexed Annuities]. The vast majority of newspaper and

magazine accounts vilify FIAs based on the results of alleged academic studies. The in-depth studies we conducted took over two years to complete and involved six Ph.D. financial economists and a pair of very well-known senior actuaries. Our studies show that the products of at least some of the companies in this field are viable – indeed, rather attractive products. Our findings regarding actual products show that since their inception in 1995, they have performed quite well – in fact, some have performed better than many alternative investment classes (corporate and government bonds, equity funds, money markets) in any combination."[3]

I couldn't put it better myself.

So…*why aren't more people talking about annuities?*

Let's look back at the 1970s – this happened to be a time when most retirees weren't thinking about annuities. Many people in the 1970s had a work-based pension, which they could supplement with Social Security income and the interest from their bank accounts. Plus, many retirees in the 1970s didn't have the life expectancy that retiring Baby Boomers anticipate today.

Let's imagine a retiree from forty or so years ago – we'll call him "George" – leaving the workforce with a full company pension, earning 10 percent interest on his bank CDs, and a life expectancy of only 10-12 years beyond retirement. He doesn't have any concerns as far as his finances go. What's George going to say if some insurance agent said to him, "Hey, you don't want that 10 percent interest on your money. You should cash in your CDs and buy a lifetime income annuity!"

George is going to tell him to take a hike – and not up Retirement Mountain either.

Obviously, George wouldn't give up that kind of reliable return on his money for something supposedly even "better." Interest rates at that time were still heading up and up, not down. The public felt comfortable with what they were doing, and many didn't consider annuities. Many thought that the company pension plan and Social Security would take care of them. Plus, if George grew up in the Depression Era and if we gave him more income he'd be looking for more coffee cans to hide it in anyway…

Those annuities that appeared in the 70s are still around – and they're called "traditional annuities." I call them antique annuities. Most people know what they are, but they aren't as efficient as the new annuity models available today. Similar to a pension decision, traditional annuities are fairly straightforward – based on your deposit and age, you would make a permanent and irrevocable income election (which is you'd decide how long you wanted your monthly payment to last, and the insurance company would decide how much you would receive each month) for retirement, or at some point down the line when you decided you wanted to begin receiving income for life. However, most people get a little nervous about making decisions that they can't change down the road if goals or needs change.

The structure of these traditional annuities wasn't the most flexible. They weren't designed to efficiently satisfy multiple goals or offer flexibility in the retiree's income strategy. However, like most good antiques, they worked, which is why they've managed to stand the test of time.

Back when they were created, annuities offered only one way to convert to guaranteed lifetime income, and that was through "annuitization." The annuitization of a contract is the process of converting a deferred asset into an immediate guaranteed income stream. There is no longer an account or contract value – only a guarantee of monthly income for the rest of your life. And while the income is for life, the decision to annuitize a contract is a permanent decision and it is irrevocable. A significant downside of traditional annuities was that if someone elected the *life-only* income option, and then passed away prior to receiving the full payout, the insurance company could keep the balance of the principal!

Which is why, at our company, we rarely use this payout option. In fact, I have used this option only *once* in my 18-year career. The sister of a 91-year-old client was moving from an independent living facility to an assisted living facility, and wanted to create the highest possible income she could get from her money. She chose a single premium immediate annuity with the "Life Only" payout option, because it almost always paid the highest income. However, the words "Life Only" also mean that the insurance company will pay this guaranteed* payment for as long as you live-regardless of how long that is. When my client's sister died, the payments stopped, and the family did not receive more payments. In this situation, since our client had no beneficiaries, this was not a factor in the decision, so this type of annuity worked very well for her and her specific needs. She received the highest payout we could offer while she was alive.

However, when it comes to the overwhelming majority of our clients, those just aren't as efficient or effective as newer models that have been specifically designed to address a wider range of more specific income goals beyond "income for life."

Remember back in the 70s when there was only one kind of telephone? Maybe you could get one in a fancy style or unusual color, but they were basically a one-size-fits-all kind of thing. They had dials instead of buttons, and you couldn't take them with you when you left the room, let alone the house, because they were attached to the wall with a long cord. Today, we have phones that go wherever we go, and that perform an amazing range of functions, from reminding us of appointments, to entertaining us, to still letting us talk to each other. That's what those annuities are like when compared to the new "models."

Today, many annuity contracts offer optional benefits (at an additional cost) that can be used to create strategies customized to fit the specific needs of more conservative-minded retirees and help them reach a wider range of retirement income goals.

CHAPTER 5

WHAT ABOUT THAT PENSION?

If you have a pension in place to fund your retirement, you should consider yourself lucky. Today, while about 80% of government employees have access to a defined retirement benefit,[4] only about 15% of corporate America does,[5] because pensions were essentially replaced by 401(k) plans or similar plans beginning around 1980.[6] Either way, pensions alone are no longer a common source of income for retirees.

Why? As *CBS MoneyWatch* explains, employers are offering pension buyouts as part of a "de-risking" strategy, which means that they are reducing their ongoing plan administration costs and lessening their concerns about their exposure to stock market volatility.[7]

Now retirees are living longer, which means that those pensions need to provide income for a longer period of time. This translates into additional expense for the corporation. Plus, the funds they have set aside and invested in the market may not have performed well enough to support the guaranteed income for life for all of the retirees under the pension who are now living longer.

In many cases, rather than continuing to manage these funds themselves, more and more companies are offering buyouts, which typically pay a lump sum to existing retirees.

In other words, they're transferring the risk – along with the responsibility of managing the money and making sure it generates the needed income – to the retiree.

Instead of the market, they turn to the safety of the insurance industry.

What does it mean when a company transfers their pension obligations to an insurance company instead of another money manager? It means that they are transferring the risk to an industry that was designed to help protect against these risks. The entire insurance industry has been built on managing risk – and, in my opinion, no industry does it better than the life insurance industry.

The life insurance industry relies on its expertise in calculating mortality. And, because they know the numbers inside out, their annuity contracts are designed to pay income for life, or in the case of life insurance, a death benefit to beneficiaries, as well as still be profitable to the company. While corporations may not have planned accordingly for expanded life expectancies of each beneficiary, the life insurance industry continues to develop products that can meet the needs of increasing longevity. In 1996, at the age of 22, I bought my first life insurance policy. The death benefit was and still is guaranteed until I reach age 120. Why? Because it's their business.

CHAPTER 6

TAKE THE PLASTIC OFF

Remember how your parents lived or are living in retirement? How about your grandparents?

Their calendars were wide open. Actually, they didn't really need calendars since it seemed like the only things they had to keep track of were grocery shopping, doctors' appointments or a trip to the bank to deposit their Social Security checks (yes, they had to deposit their own checks back then!).

That generation didn't need much because, as a whole, they didn't do as much. A generation that grew up during the Great Depression carried those hard lessons with them forever...and who could blame them?

I first began my career in financial services nearly 20 years ago in 1996, working with clients from the tail end of the Depression Generation. If someone asked me to describe my typical client back then, it wouldn't be very difficult. My clients were very conservative – in fact, they still are today – and usually lived off whatever fixed income they received.

The Depression Generation learned to save money. Even in retirement, they were still saving for a rainy day. If by chance they happened to need extra money for an unexpected expense, they didn't charge it to a credit card. These people paid cash, and if they didn't have the cash on hand and absolutely had to meet the expense, they "took interest" from a bank CD or cashed in a savings bond – something that it seemed like every retiree owned back then.

The Depression Generation retirees generally had predictable needs, goals and concerns because the financial trauma they experienced earlier in life trained them to live a certain way.

Working with this generation, I didn't get many questions about 401(k) rollovers, or required minimum distributions (RMD) from IRAs. Because most of the companies they worked for didn't even offer 401(k)s until their last few working years, while the IRA made up a very small fraction of their savings. Most of my clients had simple financial needs and an even simpler retirement goal:

Don't lose it!

When I hosted my first retirement seminar, I already knew what the people wanted to learn about because they all had the same goals, the same concerns, and the same values. So what did they want?

- They wanted to earn as much money on their savings as possible – without risking principal. As for the principal, they didn't want to touch it. Ever! A 1996 retiree's #1 question was, "Is it insured?" And when they asked it, they were referring to money in banks being guaranteed by the FDIC.

- They wanted as much money to go to their family as possible – but not yet! Only after they passed away could the kids have it.

- They wanted to make sure their beneficiaries avoided the probate court process. Most of their assets didn't have beneficiary designations, those came later.

- They wanted to make sure that nursing homes didn't eat up their savings.

These four things were the foundation of the "retirement issues" most people wanted addressed. They weren't concerned about tax laws. Most of these retirees had pension plans, savings accounts earning 5% or more and CDs earning even more than that.

The Depression Generation wanted their money to grow so they could leave more of it to their kids. They would quite literally "go without" so they could leave their kids better off financially when they passed away.

Ironically, most of their kids, who are today's Baby Boomers, didn't want their parents to go without just so they could leave them more money. They wanted their parents to enjoy the fruits of all of their labors themselves – to take that vacation, to buy that new car, to enjoy life while they could.

But it's hard to rewire someone's belief system. Those 1996 retirees were raised in a time of scarcity – so scarcity remained their primary concern.

Don't get me wrong – times may have changed, but there are some retirees out there who are still living like it's 1996. Last year, for example, I had some clients come in for an annual review. For years, I had been encouraging them to begin drawing more income from their annuities. I knew they had a modest bucket list that included some traveling and family vacations, and I had been looking forward to helping them scratch off some of those items. But they never seemed to feel comfortable spending money on themselves. They were more concerned with making sure their money would last forever.

I was surprised when we sat down for this one meeting and they said, "We've decided we are going to start doing more, we want to start spending our money. As soon as I finish my chemo, we are going to start enjoying our retirement."

"As soon as I finish my chemo…"

Those words haunted me – and made me think about my Great Aunt Irene. She too grew up during the Depression era. She spent most of her life – from age 11! – hard at work, toiling in various shoe shops and mills, working the night shift, the graveyard shift, or the early morning shift. She never made a lot of money, and she worked hard for every dollar she made.

When she wasn't working, my aunt loved to entertain family and friends, especially during the holidays. Even though she lived in a small apartment that our family barely fit into, I always looked forward to visiting Great Aunt Irene. Her gatherings were the site of many of my favorite childhood memories. She was all about FAMILY – a philosophy that affected me so strongly, it's part of what I strive for in my firm today.

I remember one year on either New Year's Day or Thanksgiving when Aunt Irene was about 56 years old. She was so excited to have us over because she had purchased a new living room set. She had been telling us about it for months and was so proud of her new furniture. She told us where she bought it and how she had selected this brand and particular set. We knew she must have been saving up for a long time, and knowing her, she probably made payments on it over time, because there was no way she could have paid for it all at once. Looking back, it was probably one of the only "brand new" things she had ever bought on her own.

When we arrived, the new furniture was on full display – a high-quality white sofa with a matching love seat. It was beautiful, and my aunt was positively beaming as she showed it off.

However, she hadn't removed the protective plastic covering from the furniture!

I just assumed it was delivered that way and she hadn't had the time to remove it. So we enjoyed our dinner and laughter and didn't give it another thought.

Until…

When we went back to Aunt Irene's next year, the furniture was still wrapped in plastic! I couldn't believe it. I asked, "Aunt Irene, why is there still plastic on your furniture?"

I'll never forget her answer.

"It's there to make it last longer."

She said it so matter-of-factly, almost like I was silly for bringing it up. She had spent so many years saving and sacrificing to buy something nice for herself that she didn't want to ruin it or wear it out. So we all sat on the floor to avoid sitting on the new furniture covered in plastic, which kind of defeated the purpose of the new furniture in the first place...

A few years later, when she was only 59 years old, Aunt Irene passed away. She was diagnosed with a brain tumor on a Monday and passed away the next Saturday. One day she had a headache and the next week she was gone.

I have probably told this story to clients and friends a hundred times over the years. Why? Because it had a big impact on me and I think it's a tale many people can connect to. When someone has been working full time since the age of 11, it's easy to understand how they might relate to money and appreciate the value of a dollar.

But, my aunt never got to fully enjoy what those dollars bought. When she died, the plastic was still on the furniture. She never got to sit on her new couch and feel the fabric and sink into those cushions.

I thought that was as such a shame.

I fully understand wanting to protect things that took years and years of hard work to obtain. But there is a big difference between protecting your assets and being afraid to enjoy them.

If I could go back in time, I would have suggested that Aunt Irene buy a lifetime warranty on the furniture – a guarantee, for a fee, that if it wore out too early, or got damaged, it would be replaced or repaired. That way, she could have enjoyed it freely.

This is one of the reasons I recommend annuities. Annuities are a guarantee.* You have worked hard to get to retirement. Insuring your retirement income with annuities in a customized strategy can provide guarantees* for life** - a lifetime "warranty" on your income.

After all, taking the plastic off of your retirement after chemo probably wasn't your original plan.

I have conducted over 10,000 interviews in my career, usually with retirees or people nearing retirement. I have NEVER had anyone tell me that they carefully saved for retirement for over 30 years so that when they finally had enough money to quit working, they could save some more.

Primarily because today's generation – at least most of it – is a little different from my Aunt Irene's generation.

Not only are today's retirees living longer – often without the perks previous generations retired with – they're also *living* differently. They want different things out of retirement than previous generations did. The vast majority of them definitely do not want to keep the plastic on their retirement nest eggs.

I call these new retirees "The Golf Cart Generation."

These retirees watched their aunts, and their parents and grandparents, scrimp and save throughout their golden years. They've decided that they want more than that. They're looking for a lifestyle that's different than how their parents spent their retirement – because these retirees have a different relationship with money. While their financial situations are more diverse and unique, most have one thing in common.

They want to enjoy their retirement NOW.

This generation wants to play – they want to compete – they want to be healthy – and they want to change the rules of retirement. They intend to go down swinging, and because they do, they are using different financial vehicles to help them meet their retirement goals.

One of my favorite authors, Malcolm Gladwell, once wrote about a town in Pennsylvania where the community was extremely tightknit. The people there were dedicated to being happy, to sharing with friends and neighbors, to anchoring themselves in the community and caring for those in need whenever they could.

It turned out that the members of this community lived longer and healthier lives than the people in almost any other place on earth.

I believe the Golf Cart Generation has a lot in common with the citizens of that Pennsylvania town. Because of that, they're not only rewriting the rules of retirement, I believe they will also rewrite the life-expectancy tables.

The Golf Cart Generation wants to retire on their own terms. They don't want to be concerned about money the way their parents were. They want to be more financially confident in knowing that if they take care of themselves and stay true to their core values, they can afford to live well into their 90s and 100s. At the same time, they want to be sure they will not outlive their retirement assets.

I have called The Villages, Florida home since January of 2000 – a town that has been dubbed the "nation's fastest-growing metro area" by the *Orlando Sentinel* and ranked by *Forbes* in 2012 as "the No. 1 fastest-growing small town."

A lot of those new residents are also new retirees.

When I meet a couple for the first time, I always ask them "The Question":

"So, how'd you end up in The Villages?"

And then I get "The Answer."

"Well," they might say, "we saw an ad on TV and they were offering these great packages on a one week vacation….it was cheap! For something like $600 they put us up in an amazing place and they gave us some money that we could spend inside the 'bubble.' We went dancing and played golf and they took us on a tour. They showed us this game you play with pickles and balls…and before we left we bought a $250,000 villa."

Wait…what? From pickles and balls to an investment of $250k? That's the most expensive "cheap" vacation most of us will ever experience!

But for the people I work with who've made The Villages their home, it's worth every penny. The reason? I believe it's the lifestyle. I see them living lives that are healthier, more active and have more recreational options and more spiritual purpose than the lives of many 20, 30 or 40-somethings.

This is the opposite of what your parents experienced when they retired. Were their lives about joining social clubs and team sports and planning fun activities? Were their day planners packed with activities like mahjong, woodworking, softball, polo, Parrotheads, the Ohio Club and the Italian-American or Irish organization? Maybe they didn't even have a day planner. For many of our parents, life was focused on saving for a "rainy day."

Which sometimes made it hard to enjoy the days that were sunny.

But today, in places like The Villages, there are thousands of clubs for retirees to choose from. And then there's golf, which seems to be at the heart of everything.

What would your parents and grandparents have thought about going to the doctor, grocery shopping and making a bank deposit if they could have tooled around in their own golf cart?

It kind of changes your whole perspective on things, doesn't it?

Here's the thing. If you don't want to retire like your parents, then using your retirement assets in the same way – with the same old strategies that worked in the past – doesn't make sense. Just putting your money in the bank and forgetting about it won't get you very far with interest rates at near-record lows.

What you need is a retirement income strategy that actually fits your financial goals. For some, this may mean using annuities to guarantee* a portion of your income, so that it will never be outlived.** This leaves you with a couple of choices. You can focus on a ***distribution*** strategy that will provide the income you need to enjoy for yourself and with your family while you're living, allowing you to make memories together and enjoy a rich retirement lifestyle. Or you can stick with an ***accumulation*** strategy. Either strategy is fine if it supports the lifestyle you want to focus on. When you were imagining what retirement would be, and you were saving and accumulating, what did retirement look like to you? Those are questions only you can answer.

CHAPTER 7

INCOME FOR LIVING

Everybody loves sports, right?

Well, maybe not everybody, but there's something about the way sports are structured that just makes sense. Which is why, when I sit down with my clients to discuss how insurance products, including annuities, can be used to help them prepare for their retirement, I like to use a sports analogy to break down the three phases of retirement.

I call them:

- The First Half
- The Second Half
- Overtime

Each stage of the retirement game is different – and since each stage is different, each requires a different strategy to help ensure that you can continue to enjoy the life you want to live.

FIRST HALF = LIVING... DO IT NOW!

I call the First Half the "DO IT NOW" stage of retirement. Why? Because this is when retirees are most healthy, fit and excited to finally not be working! Now is the time to start checking those big things off your bucket list – the cruises, the road trips across the U.S., the travels to Europe, or maybe just spending more time with your extended family.

Of course, activities like these cost money. In the First Half of retirement, your cost of living may actually go up because of consumption.

Living is what this First Half of retirement is all about – you're doing as much *living* as you possibly can! That's one of the distinctions I like to address in your retirement income plan – income for life vs. income for living. This is a strategy that allows you to live a full life in your "DO IT NOW" years.

During the First Half, our goal is to use annuities to increase your income so you have more than you need to cover your expenses. This provides you with an income flow that is guaranteed by the issuing carriers, which can allow you some flexibility in how you spend your money. But that doesn't mean you're going to spend it all!

Look at it this way: If the cost of gasoline is $4 a gallon and I give you enough for $12 a gallon, does that mean you're automatically going to search for the most expensive gas available? Of course not. "Front-loading" your income strategy simply means that you have some options to choose from. You have more income than you probably need so you can spend some now – and continue to save some for later. We are always mindful of your financial goals and your situation; we would never suggest living more for today if it meant jeopardizing your financial future in later years. In many instances, we discover that retirees actually under-spend in the first half of their retirement years because they are concerned about running out of income later. This means they are often times missing out on doing things today – making memories – by saving their assets for when they get into their later retirement years. Do you think you will be healthier and more motivated in the first 10-15 years of retirement or following the 10-15 years?

Eventually the first phase of retirement will end. Maybe it will be a question of health, or energy level, or having checked enough of those bucket list items off.

SECOND HALF = AND...RELAX!

That's when you move into the Second Half – what I call the "BEEN THERE, DONE THAT" stage of retirement.

This is the stage where most retirees want to relax more or stay close to home. Maybe it's getting harder to walk all over Greece and Italy. Maybe you don't want to sit through another 13-hour plane ride. Or maybe you're just content to enjoy life and family right where you are.

In this second phase, the primary concern is financial confidence, and ensuring the longevity of your retirement assets. You want to make sure you have enough money to live, and that your money will last for the rest of your life. Of course you may want enough money to fly the grandkids down for a visit, or to take that occasional cruise with friends, if one comes up ... regardless of where it's going! But mostly, the Second Half is about *MORE FINANCIAL CONFIDENCE.* So that's what we focus on.

OVERTIME = INDEPENDENCE

Finally, we move into Overtime stage of retirement, which is a different story. As much as you love your kids and grandkids, you probably don't want to move in with them, right? "OT" is about staying *independent.* In addition to receiving guaranteed income throughout your life – which is all the way to the end of the retirement game – another way to help address the complexities and expense of living a lot longer than you might expect is through life insurance. The primary purpose for life insurance is to provide a death benefit to your beneficiaries. The proceeds can be used to go to your spouse for income replacement or your children and grandchildren as a gift in the event of your death.

In addition to the death benefit, some types of life insurance may offer living benefit riders that allow you to accelerate the death benefit early, and while you're still living. Some life insurance policies allow you to access the death benefits for daily living expenses and healthcare costs—of course, certain conditions must be met, but these contracts are growing in popularity and may add value to your overall strategy. Working with an insurance agent that understands these contracts is very important in the decision making process.

It's also worth noting that life insurance has some of the most attractive tax benefits in the current tax code – death benefits are generally distributed income tax free, cash accumulation inside the contracts generally grows tax-deferred, and can be accessed on a tax-free or tax-favored basis.

There are several types of life insurance contracts. They may be complicated and can be expensive, but I love life insurance! When suitable for you, they are worth every penny, and can offer a wide range of benefits. However, I could write an entire book on the complexities of life insurance. Be sure to talk to an insurance professional about the different types and options to help you determine a policy that fits your needs. Please take your time and be careful purchasing life insurance, especially if you're at or nearing retirement. Remember, when you're retired and at the top of Retirement Mountain, some mistakes can be more significant.

An important aspect of the First Half, Second Half and Overtime strategy is giving you a game plan for a retirement strategy that can help you live your life. It's your life, and it should be lived your way.

I know retirees often don't feel confident spending their "extra" First Half money until they know they have measures in place to help them remain financially confident throughout the Second Half, and be able to remain *independent* if they reach Overtime years down the road. If we don't include a strategy for the end of the game up front, it doesn't matter how much income you receive at the beginning. If you aren't confident that you will have financial vehicles to help carry you through the end of the game, you'll probably be concerned about enjoying it now.

Financial professionals can work with you to help you achieve more of your financial goals throughout your life. As financial professionals, our job is to make sure you have financial vehicles to help carry you through the end of the game. There's a real art to designing a customized income strategy. It starts with identifying and understanding your goals and concerns, and then making sure that those goals and concerns are addressed in the strategy that we design together.

For example, your biggest concern might be, "What will happen if my spouse passes away and there's a drop in income?" If you aren't 100% sure you've protected your spouse down the road, you may not be comfortable enjoying the First Half portion of your retirement.

I can't tell you how many times the husband will tell me that his primary concern is making sure that there will be enough money for his wife and family when he passes away. If we address this issue head-on, we may be able to eliminate the risk with life insurance. Wouldn't it be nice to know that you could spend as much money as you want to on those "extras," like more travel or flying the grandkids down, no matter how long you live, and know that the ones you care about most will be taken care of financially when you're gone? That's what retirement is all about—that's what my company is all about!

That's why we start with a plan to help you design a strategy: one that looks down the road, and work our way backwards to the present. In a way, we reverse engineer your retirement strategy. We start with Overtime planning, then Second Half strategies, which leaves everyone with a much better view of what the First Half could look like. Then we look to find the right life insurance and annuity products that can be used to help meet your retirement needs.

CHAPTER 8

SEAT BELTS

What do seat belts have to do with retirement income planning?

If you're old enough to be thinking about retirement, you can probably remember when wearing a seatbelt was optional. In fact, I'll bet you can remember a time when you could ride in a car without sitting in a seat. My sister and I used to beg our parents to let us sit in the "way back" in our station wagon as kids.

What were our parents thinking? Actually, they were thinking like everybody else…that it was no big deal to have the kids rolling around loose in a car.

Back then, a lot of people refused to wear safety belts, even if their car had them. Some weren't comfortable wearing them or thought that without a seat belt holding them down, they could use their arms to stop themselves from being tossed around.

Really?

Some people may have believed it was safer NOT to wear a seatbelt if you were in a crash. They claimed that if you were in an accident, wearing a seat belt would hinder you from escaping the automobile. What if the car caught on fire? Or if you were trapped under water?

Where I grew up, in Maine, ice fishing is a popular activity in the winter. Sadly, every year, there would be at least one tragedy where someone would drive their car on the frozen lake, fall through the ice, and be trapped in their car – with horrible results. Invariably, some people would blame the fact that the victims were wearing seat belts, claiming that, if not for those pesky seat belts, the victims might have escaped.

Me? I don't think the seat belts were the real problem.

The fact is, as we get older, the joy of riding in the "way back" goes away, and most of us discover we actually prefer the security of sitting in actual seats with our safety belts fastened.

The research on the effectiveness of seatbelts has proved our older, wiser selves are right. It's clear that seat belts save lives, to the point where the subject is rarely debated anymore. In fact, in most states, wearing a seat belt is now the law.

Which brings me to the answer to the question I asked at the beginning of this chapter: What do seat belts have to do with retirement income planning?

Well, cars aren't the only things that crash. As we've learned several times over the past few decades, markets do too. As you get older and still have funds in the stock market, market declines can have a greater impact on your lifestyle and the longevity of your retirement assets, basically because you don't have enough time to make them up.

That's where fixed index annuities, when used properly, can be like seat belts for your finances. They can help protect your retirement from economic fender benders and crashes to help protect the assets you need on the road ahead. Because they are tied to an external index but without exposure to the market itself, fixed index annuities allow for potential growth when the market is high, and your principal and prior gains are protected from loss when the market turns downward. They are designed to protect a portion of your retirement assets from market fluctuations, and help provide a guaranteed* income for the rest of your life.** Remember, annuities are also subject to limitations, surrender charges and holding periods, but they can be powerful tools for providing benefits in retirement. A financial professional can help you find an annuity that is appropriate for your retirement assets.

That's why I've been helping clients design retirement strategies using various fixed annuities and fixed index annuities since 1996. And yes, during that same period, our stock markets have seen extraordinary growth and reached all-time highs – several times, in fact. But, remember what I learned on Longs Peak – what goes up must come down. For many retirees, who suffered through the bursting of the dot-com bubble, and/or the real estate and banking collapse, that lesson was extremely painful. Some people lost a majority of the money they'd been saving for decades. And the reality is, no one really knows what the stock market will do.

Since I only use fixed and fixed index annuities in my retirement strategies, my clients have walked away from every market crash and economic downturn unscathed – they haven't lost a dime in any of the annuity strategies or products they've owned due to market fluctuations – ever!

That's why I look at annuities as a metaphorical safety belt for you and your retirement strategy. Since they can guarantee* an income for life** no matter how long you live, they can provide a measure of security throughout your retirement years. They were created to help protect your assets from those unexpected, economic fender benders.

There is nothing else like an annuity, because there is simply no other vehicle designed for the sole purpose of guaranteeing* income for a specific time period, or for life,** regardless of interest rates or how long you live. Nothing else provides a seat belt for your retirement like annuities can. No other product provides those guarantees* for life.**

Let me say that again – because it's that important:

THERE IS NO OTHER INSTRUMENT THAT PAYS GUARANTEED* INCOME FOR LIFE.**

And that's regardless of interest rates, market performance or how long you live, which means you can relax and enjoy the ride.

Now, let's think about this current generation of retirees again. With life expectancy tables stretching into the 90s and beyond, one of this generation's biggest fears is that they will "outlive their money."

How can there not be serious consideration for using annuities as a part of your income strategy? Seat belts and annuities. Neither one is very flashy but both can provide valuable benefits when used properly. They should be considered for "part" of your plan but not all of it. Remember, annuities are long-term vehicles to help protect a portion of your retirement assets.

CHAPTER 9

DO YOU HAVE THE RIGHT TEAM?

"Golf is the closest game to the game we call life. You get bad breaks from good shots; you get good breaks from bad shots – but you have to play the ball as it lies."

~ Bobby Jones, *American amateur golfer and co-founder of the Masters Tournament*

As I've pointed out, annuities can be an effective financial tool when it comes to designing a retirement strategy. However, because there are different types of annuities and annuities can have different options, choosing the right annuity to help achieve your retirement goals can seem overwhelming. Since I'm now working with the Golf Cart Generation, I like to compare the process of choosing the right annuity to golf.

Some people will say, "Choosing annuities? But aren't all annuities the same?"

The Tools

Theoretically an annuity is an annuity, just as a golf club is a golf club. But the most successful golfers use clubs that have been customized to their game and their way of playing. Don't believe me? Try using someone else's golf clubs in your next round, then let me know how well you score. Chances are, you will recognize if the club feels right to you immediately.

The key is customization. Your retirement strategy using annuities (or any other financial instrument) needs to be tailored to fit your needs and customized to fit the way you live. Too often I see people in my office who were "sold" a single annuity or several annuities, and after just a few minutes of talking about their goals, their lifestyle, their family and their money, I realize they weren't "fitted" with the right instruments. They were sold something generic right off the shelf. Unless your annuity fits your financial needs, it could be like trying to play golf with someone else's clubs.

However, as any golfer will tell you, the right clubs alone won't make you the next Tiger Woods or Rory McIlroy. You also need to know how to use them. There's a big difference between hitting a golf ball into a net at the local sporting goods store, or off a plastic mat on the practice range, and learning how to properly use your clubs on the fairways.

Our customized strategies use multiple annuities that are offered by top rated insurance companies, which have long track records of financial strength. We do not create or design our own annuities; we help you select features, riders, and appropriate contracts to fit your stated goals.

The Basics

Understanding the basics of golf is the foundation for building a successful game. There are many considerations: your grip, your stance, proper alignment, and keeping your head down. These are all important in learning how to consistently swing a club successfully.

Understanding the basics of annuities is just as important. Today's annuities offer a wide selection of features and benefits to choose from. So how do you determine which products and features would work well for you?

Like a good golf instructor, we like to start with the basics. We call it *Annuities 101*. This is the foundation for building your understanding of annuities, including optional riders, and how they can be used effectively in a retirement income strategy and planning.

In golf, there are also a lot of rules – in fact, there is a whole book of them. Knowing how to apply those rules before you go out on the course can give you a strong advantage. Again, annuities are no different. Annuities have rules, and understanding them before you buy them will help you to determine if an annuity meets your needs, and which benefits will work best for you.

Once you have the appropriate clubs for you and understand the rules of the game, you're ready to head out on the course and play, right?

Not quite.

The Caddy

If you have ever played golf you know all too well that selecting clubs and avoiding hazards are useful, and in some cases, necessary, to having an enjoyable and successful round. A great caddy will offer the best guidance they can that complements you and your game to give you the best chance to win. And again, retirement is not much different. Just as a golf caddy may suggest a wedge, 5-iron or driver, a "retirement caddy" can help you select the most appropriate annuities to accomplish your short-range, mid-range, and long-range retirement income goals.

My company, Parady Financial, gets the majority of our business from referrals and client endorsements. We feel that when our clients succeed, we do too. If we can help you avoid the retirement "hazards," then maybe we'll get a chance to "caddy" for your friends and family in the future.

The Swing Coach

The greatest golfers in the world never, ever go it alone. They still take lessons in between tournaments, and they rarely play in a major tournament without their swing coach by their side.

A highly-trained and experienced swing coach can guide a golfer through any challenges that might pop up during play. They coach their golfers through the tough times, and this advice and support can be invaluable.

A personal swing coach not only has an in-depth understanding of their client's golfing mechanics and tendencies, he or she will also have a detailed knowledge of the golfer's psyche. The coach is there at the most crucial moments in a player's career – because those are the times when small adjustments can make the difference between winning and losing.

In retirement, we believe that having a "coach" who knows you and your tendencies, your family, your assets and your core values can provide the best advice and guidance when you need it the most. This is why you have trained and experienced financial professionals – for the tough times. Nobody needs help when they always hit the fairways and greens and make all the putts. We need professionals when conditions change, and we are faced with challenging situations.

Ongoing Training – The Learning Lounge

Most recreational golfers don't have access to all the professional assistance I've described above – which is probably at least part of the reason why average golfers admire how well the pros play.

But when it comes to your retirement, you do have access to a team of financial professionals with specific areas of focused training. Those professionals can be crucial to helping you navigate your way through the entire process, from choosing your annuity, to helping you learn how to use those instruments, to dealing with the ups and downs of life and adjustments as your needs and goals change.

At Parady Financial, we've created a space we call the Parady Learning Lounge. It is dedicated to providing information about our services, products we offer and other retirement issues. Our

Learning Lounge is located in our Clubhouse where our clients and friends can learn about different facets of the "game" of retirement in a relaxing social and group environment.

We offer full complimentary access to all Learning Lounge topics and sessions that we conduct. We bring in guest speakers to discuss topics outside our areas of specific knowledge, and encourage our clients to attend as many presentations as they like even before they make a commitment.

Ultimately, this is your retirement lifestyle at stake, so we think it's important to get you fitted with the appropriate tools. We can help you learn the basics on how to use life insurance and annuities, and we provide that all-important "retirement caddy" to help you along the way.

Keep in mind, over time your game and life goals may change. The golf clubs you carried 30 years ago probably are not the same clubs you use today. (By the way, if your 3-wood is still made out of actual wood, we should talk immediately!) Our process of sharing information allows our clients to learn about the latest products and strategies as they become available, so they can always be on top of their game.

Of course, no one becomes a championship golfer after just a few lessons. Our model is designed to allow you to go at your own pace and get information through a process of osmosis. We believe gradual absorption of complicated retirement issues and insurance-related strategies is a much better approach – and more effective – than a single sales pitch.

Now, consider this:
Imagine that every time you play a round of golf, your game improves. You hit more fairways, more greens, and you have fewer putts per round. And this continues for months or even years. Each time you are out on the course is better than the last. But every time you walk off the 18th green, there is a golf club sales representative waiting, trying to sell you a set of the latest and greatest clubs, trying to replace the ones you already have.

Since you are playing well, you probably have no interest in changing anything. Then one day, you fall into a slump. Everything stops going your way. Your drives fly out of bounds and you can't make a putt to save your life. Frustrated, confused, and emotional about your game, you finish your round and there's that sales rep again.

What kind of decision do you think you'll make when you're feeling emotional and frustrated? It is almost never a good idea to make big decisions under stress or when you're emotionally charged. Decisions about your retirement shouldn't be made quickly or when under duress either. One of the mistakes a retiree can make is a snap or emotional decision when life is not going your way. No matter how noble the intentions, a decision made from a place of frustration, anger, or fear almost never turns out to be smart in the long run.

It's also valuable to note that changing clubs isn't always the right answer. Maybe it isn't always the club? Sometimes all you need is a lesson, a meeting with your swing coach to steer you in the right direction.

CHAPTER 10

MORE INCOME? NO THANKS...?

Everybody loves income, right?

But "deferred income"? That may be different story.

One type of annuity that people own today are "deferred annuities," which means during the accumulation phase, interest is growing tax-deferred. Then during the distribution phase, the interest that is paid to you is taxed. It's not uncommon for people to own annuities and keep them in the deferral phase in to their mid-to-late 70s. Not because this is the way they want it, or that it still makes sense to defer the payout, but they often don't know how to make their annuities work for them.

I think it's important to understand that at the core, annuities are intended to provide income. This can be income *now* or income *later*.

But, why do so many people continue deferring income with their annuities? They would never have done that with a raise from their boss.

It comes down to knowing and understanding how to use your annuities to your best advantage. Let's think about what this means for you.

If you had an option today – right this minute – to begin receiving income for the rest of your life, how many more days, weeks, or years would you want to wait before you began to collect?

Let me rephrase the question: How many people chose to take social security at age 62? How about age 66? How about the maximum monthly payout offered at age 70?

A few of my clients waited until age 70 to begin collecting Social Security benefits. It's true that the later you wait, the bigger the monthly benefit. But it's also true that you will receive that benefit for a shorter period of time.

In this respect, annuity payouts work in a similar way. Annuities will generally pay-out a higher amount per month the later you begin your income payments, but the trade-off is that you will receive the income for a shorter period of time.

Annuities don't just sit there like Aunt Irene's furniture with the plastic on it. Annuity payments can be used as a tool to help supplement your lifestyle and goals, or to purchase other financial or insurance instruments.

When you have an annuity that will provide a stream of income for life,[**] you're in control of how to use those funds. You can decide if you need a smaller amount of income for a longer period of time or a larger amount of income for a shorter period of time. As financial professionals, we can help you determine which annuity strategies may suit your needs for the first half, second half and overtime in your retirement.

I meet a lot of people that already own annuities and aren't taking the income from them. It is a source of great frustration for me because if you're in retirement and you own an annuity contract that guarantees income and you're not taking the income yet, why did you buy it? Of course, annuities must be suitable for each individual's needs, but remember, annuities can pay you income for the rest of your life. When you own something that will pay you forever, how many more years do you want to wait before you start collecting those payments?

CHAPTER 11

GET IT IN WRITING!

I am now going to introduce you to "four little words" that are powerful and will help prevent you from uttering some unpleasant "four letter words" down the road – especially when it comes to your retirement income planning.

What are they?

"Get it in writing!"

Since I began my career back in 1996, I've probably conducted more than 10,000 interviews with retirees about their retirement strategies, dreams and concerns. A lot of these people already had a "financial person" advising them about their money.

But none of them had any written plans.

That's right. None. Zero. I literally cannot recall ever seeing a single financial or retirement income plan that was presented to me in writing. Not once in over 10,000 meetings has a prospective client come into my office, shown me a written retirement strategy and asked me what I thought about it.

To be clear, I'm not talking about an insurance illustration or an industry-regulated prospectus. People bring those in every day. But those aren't strategies for how to use your money.

What I mean by a written plan is a written strategy specifically designed to help you, the client, understand where your assets are and what you may be able to expect in return. As you might imagine, a tool like that could be very helpful.

It's hard enough choosing a team of financial professionals to help you accomplish your retirement goals. Insurance and annuities can be difficult products to understand. Policies and contracts are written in legal terms – or "legalese," which can be confusing and challenging to understand.

That's why I make sure each and every one of my clients receives a formal, written document, in plain English, explaining how their retirement strategy is designed to work.

Talk is cheap – and let's face it, one of the hardest things to do is trust the words that are spoken in a conference room, especially when an agent or professional is trying to convince you that they have all the answers for your personal financial situation. Sometimes I worry about what is being said to solicit business. However, I worry a lot more about what isn't being said, disclosed or discussed in those meetings.

Often, people don't know the right questions to ask. How could they? But since you don't always know what to ask, how can you be sure you're getting all the information you need to make an appropriate decision about your financial future?

My purpose here is not to beat up on the "other" financial representatives out there. It's not easy to understand and explain everything the client needs to know in just a few meetings. And even if they have a good system in place to educate their clients, a one, two, or even three-person financial team has their hands full when it comes to covering everything that goes into designing a comprehensive, tax-efficient strategy. It's hard to be knowledgeable about a variety of topics and still find the time to *listen* to your clients' goals, concerns and desires.

That's why, at Parady Financial, we take a unique approach to helping people in retirement. We recognize the fact that everyone has different goals, concerns and objectives they want to accomplish with their retirement strategy. We take the time to listen to your needs, and then we work to find the right products to help you design a comprehensive, efficient retirement strategy.

We have a number of highly educated professionals on our "planning team", which at the time of this writing consists of two Investment Advisor Representatives, four Certified Public Accountants (CPAs), two Certified Financial Planners (CFPs), one Certified Annuity Specialist and five Licensed Insurance agents with life insurance and annuity licenses in Florida and Colorado.

In our approach with clients, we typically take them on a two to three month educational journey to accomplish three important things:

1. We want to understand what's important to our clients – and this takes time!

2. We want our clients to understand the insurance products and strategies we use. This includes the pros and cons of the products. We also work closely with our affiliate company, Parady Tax Solutions, to understand the possible tax implications. We think taxes are the name of the game, which is why we have a CPA and a CFP on staff, and they can be involved in tax implications in the design of your strategy if needed.

3. We always make sure you "get it in writing!" Yes, here are those four little words again. Before you buy anything from us, you get it in writing – a plain English summary of how we intend to have the recommended annuity products work together to help meet your retirement goals and address your concerns, as well as information on the terms and conditions of the various products.

Taken together, we think these three distinctions make Parady Financial unique. We are willing to take responsibility for the recommendations that we make about your financial future.

If you already have a written retirement strategy – let me be the first to say, congratulations!! And if you don't, why not? What's keeping you from getting one? There's a lot at stake – your retirement future!

CHAPTER 12

I HATE TAXES!

CONTRIBUTED BY
KATHIE LASETER, CPA, CFP®
& LICENSED INSURANCE AGENT

Yes, I hate taxes. Most people do.

I hear these words every single day. And to be honest, taxes usually aren't a fun subject to write, talk, or even think about – let alone pay. But they aren't going anywhere. They can be a huge piece of your retirement income planning puzzle that need to be dealt with.

Why?

When people tell me how much they hate paying taxes, I usually remind them that they may actually like what they're paying today compared to what they might be paying in the future. This is especially true for people whose retirement savings have been growing in a tax-deferred venue like an IRA/401(k) or deferred annuities.

Those assets are specifically designed to grow tax-deferred – which means you can delay paying income taxes until the money is withdrawn at a later date – under the assumption that when you take the money out or pass it on to your family, you or they will be in a lower tax bracket than you were in your working years.

There's also an assumption that your total tax liability will be lower in the future. Which begs the question, does anyone still believe that there is any chance that we will all be paying lower taxes in the future than we are today?

Before I go any further, I would like to state, for the record, that I actually like being in a position to pay taxes. I clearly remember a time in my life when I didn't owe the government any tax on my income, because I wasn't making any money! Of course, like most of us, I'd like to see some of the decision-makers in Washington make better choices on how and where they allocate our tax-money. Our country is facing some serious issues. For instance, we know that currently:

- **Medicare is underfunded.**[8]
- **Social Security is underfunded.**[9]
- **Thousands of Baby Boomers retire every day** – adding to those Medicare and Social Security issues.
- **Our aging population has increasing longevity** – those retiring Baby Boomers are projected to live longer than ever.

Now, I'm not an expert on economics, but the way I see it, there are three basic ways to address these problems:

1. Cut spending
2. Cut benefits
3. Raise taxes

Option three is my biggest concern. Because it isn't just about raising taxes, which are historically very low right now, it's the potential for a one-two punch of raising taxes AND cutting benefits!

What if you need to draw more of your money in retirement to cover healthcare costs or to supplement Medicare benefits? And at the time you need to draw that extra money, the tax rates are 10% higher, or more? The combination of options two and three together could have a significant impact on your nest egg, your lifestyle, and your financial confidence in retirement.

And it could happen.

The fact is that most of the wealth in America is owned by or controlled by YOU, the Baby Boomers and retirees of America.[10]

Of course, you can't do anything about the way you saved your money up to now. What you can do is have a strategy in place to address the potential for higher income taxes in the future.

A lot of people don't give much thought to this issue. Many times in my career I've sat down with someone who is genuinely concerned about protecting money from stock market volatility and they want to learn about annuities — or they've already purchased an annuity from another agent to protect their money from potential stock market losses. We feel it is important to work with qualified CPAs and tax advisors to review your strategy so that it also takes taxes into consideration.

After all, if you save your money from potential stock market losses but then you end up owing more in taxes, what's the point?

We believe tax strategies are absolutely crucial to all retirement income plans, especially if you have a portion of assets held in tax-deferred instruments such as IRAs, 401(k)s, TSP, 457s or 403(b)s. We have a team of CPAs on staff at Parady Financial Group to help address tax concerns and look for tax planning opportunities for our clients.

CHAPTER 13

IRA TAX STRATEGIES

The following is for informational purposes only. It is not intended to provide tax or legal advice. We encourage you to discuss your situation with a qualified tax advisor or attorney.

We do not provide guidance on securities holding. Be sure to consult your registered representative or investment advisor regarding your securities.

IRAs account for about 25% of all retirement assets in America.[11]

That's a lot.

Many of you reading this book may have one or have decided to put your money into them.

That's great.

But, do you have a plan for how to make withdrawals from them?

Having an exit strategy for using the funds from an IRA for various goals can provide a measure of flexibility against the impact of taxes.

Let's back up a minute and talk about the purpose of IRAs.

As most of you probably know, they're designed to help grow your money without being taxed until you get to retirement. In other words, they're designed for accumulation without taxation along the way, and they're based on the assumption that when you do withdraw the funds, you'll likely be in a lower tax bracket than when you were working.

If you don't have a plan in place, it may result in unintended tax consequences for you, or possibly your beneficiaries.

As these instruments grow untaxed in order to more provide income during retirement, it is required that you begin withdrawing IRA money when you reach the age of 70 ½ and they are taxed as ordinary income. These are called Required Minimum Distributions (RMDs) and are based on your life expectancy and the amounts residing in IRAs.

Now, it's common for people to only take out what they *have* to take out when they *have* to take it out – in other words, the very minimum amount required. They do that because they hate paying taxes – and because they also like to watch their IRAs continue to get bigger.

But that can end up being a Catch-22, as they may be setting themselves and/or their beneficiaries up for more taxes down the line.

It's what we call the "deferred dilemma."

The more your IRA grows, the bigger potential you, or your beneficiaries, may have of paying a much larger tax in the future. Now, when I say that to a client, the answer is frequently, "Well, I'm leaving the money to my kids, so what?" Here's the problem. If you end up with an IRA worth $500,000 or more and that money gets passed on to a beneficiary, be it your kids or a spouse, that beneficiary is going to end up paying a lot more taxes on the money than you would have paid if you simply withdrew income from the IRA strategically, with smaller amounts per year while you were alive. You still pay taxes on the distribution, but it will be in smaller amounts. And as with annuities, you can take distributions to fund other financial vehicles.

In other words, you avoided taking out bigger amounts because you didn't want to pay taxes on it. But all you did was cause your beneficiaries to pay more taxes on the full amount they received.

One of the big reasons we created a separate tax firm, Parady Tax Solutions LLC, was to help clients with this specific issue. We built our tax firm to provide comprehensive solutions to help our clients realize tax savings over the entire lifespan of their IRAs. The bottom line here is that IRAs are not designed to transfer wealth and are probably the absolute *last* thing that you want to leave to your children, because that money will be taxed as ordinary income, and will likely push them into a higher, or possibly the highest, tax bracket. Now, if you don't need that IRA income during your retirement, there are other ways to move that money into other tax-free or tax-favored positions. We at Parady Financial can work in concert with these professionals to help bring a long-term strategy to the table.

For example, you can take distributions from the IRAs to fund life insurance, which happens to have some of the most advantageous tax benefits in our tax code. As we mentioned in earlier chapters, life insurance, when used properly, provides for a death benefit that can be passed directly to beneficiaries, income tax free. (Be careful of how much life insurance and of who owns your life insurance, because the death benefits could be added to your estate value and be subject to an "estate tax." As stated earlier, we could write an entire book on life insurance.)

The thing to remember is that life insurance today is different and often more flexible than the life insurance your parents might have had in place. In addition to providing a death benefit, which is the primary purpose of life insurance, some policies offer "living advantages" through accumulation of cash value. There can also be optional features (some with an additional fee), known as riders, which can be added on to the policy. These riders can provide for additional benefits if certain conditions are met. For example, similar to annuities, life insurance can be a valuable product that can be funded with IRA and non-IRA distributions.

But, if you don't work with a team of various professionals, you might never know how to do those things. You might end up passing on a huge tax bill to your beneficiaries or passing up some tax advantages while you're living.

As I've discussed a great deal in this book, you should *always* work with a team of different financial professionals – insurance agents, CPAs, financial planners, attorneys, and others that are able to bring a long-term strategy to the table. This is particularly crucial with a married couple. We will always work on creating a financial road map for where they both want to go while they're both living. If you are still married, we think the best time to create a succession strategy is together.

Just as important is planning for the eventuality that something will happen to one of the spouses – leaving the other to make decisions without their life partner. You want to plan for this while you're both living, you're both healthy and you can think things through in a cool, collected way. That way, when the worst does happen, you're not trying to *create* a plan from scratch when you're in a highly charged and emotional state. Instead, you're simply *implementing* a strategy that has already been created and reviewed every three or four months by you, for you, with your team of professionals. There's a big difference between implementing a strategy and creating a new strategy.

There's no harm in planning – and there can be a lot of risk in not planning. Again, you don't want your retirement to be about risk. You want it to be about enjoying life.

Planning is the way to help give you confidence to do just that.

CHAPTER 14

IT TAKES MORE THAN A MEAL

There's no such thing as a free lunch. Or, for that matter, a free steak dinner.

There are a lot of retirement "seminars" being held in rooms in steakhouses, where a company or consultant will feed you after you listen to their pitch. Most of them are selling specific products. And they might be good products.

But what happens when the dinner is over? We believe good information involves more than just a free steak dinner at a hotel or clubhouse. It is an ongoing process. You should be meeting with your insurance agent, or other financial professionals, on a regular basis (monthly, quarterly, or yearly, depending on your needs) and be exposed to the retirement tools and resources that they can offer to help you be sure your financial needs are being met.

Retirement strategies can evolve. A one-shot seminar should be the beginning of a process, not the end of it. There are many complex issues for today's retiree to consider. Just the fact that life expectancy has increased so dramatically brings new factors that need to be taken into account. Products change, and life changes.

That's one of the reasons we created our own dedicated "Learning Lounge," where our clients get information about what they need to know, where they can have open, honest and meaningful conversations about their retirement income planning strategies, and where they have the ability to be trained, coached and mentored by knowledgeable professionals in the various topics that are presented.

Our Learning Lounge is also a relaxed venue where newcomers can come and spend time with existing clients. They are able to mix and mingle with others who are at different stages in the learning process and get valuable perspectives and information they might otherwise miss. Again, it's an ongoing process that allows clients the time and space to learn at their own pace. It also allows our existing clients to get a refresher course or catch up on new products or emerging trends.

We also host quarterly reviews for our clients only, which we call "Parady State of the Nations," featuring talks on the overall state of the insurance industry, the existing products we use, new products and financial strategies as well as upcoming Parady events. We also keep current and prospective clients up-to-date on any changes or expansions that are occurring at Parady Financial Group. We believe communication is the key to any successful relationship, and we feel we have created a unique way to ensure that successful communication is always happening.

Finally, we like to bring in speakers to add outside and authoritative voices from the financial industry to the conversation. We have hosted: Ed Slott, named "The Best Source for IRA Advice" by *The Wall Street Journal*; Mick Higley, publisher of *By The Numbers*; and Craig Pearlman, Esq., a renowned Estate Planning/ Probate Attorney.

We do this because we believe our clients should only choose retirement strategies after they fully understand their options. And it's our experience that our clients do, in fact, appreciate the informal and informative presentations we offer.

Remember, there's no such thing as a free lunch. At our Learning Lounge you will always get information that is relevant and up-to-date in a venue for ongoing education about financial strategies that our clients consider to be priceless.

CHAPTER 15

ABOUT PARADY FINANCIAL

When I tell people about my childhood, I sometimes think it's ironic that I didn't always aspire to a career in the financial services industry. But, once I shifted gears and began working in insurance, I realized that the struggles my family experienced during my preteen and teen years were crucial to who I would become.

Looking back, it seems clear that growing up with so much uncertainty and anxiety around health and money issues probably attracted me to helping people. It turned out to be a natural fit for me – I understood the very same concerns many of my clients had *because I had lived them*. I understood their fears of loss. And it felt especially rewarding to be able to help those clients achieve a measure of financial confidence that my family was never able to enjoy. It's like I was being trained my entire life for a career of helping people live the retirement they want.

Living and working in The Villages – a community that has grown from 18,000 people when I moved here to over 110,000 – provides the perfect home base for me. It's a place where I can be of service to a wide range of wonderful people – many of whom I feel fortunate to call a part of our family at Parady Financial.

In fact, the concept of family is a core philosophy at Parady Financial. It's so important that when you walk into our office it's the first thing you see, right there in big script letters on the wall over the aquarium. *"We are Family."* It's been this way since 2008, when I partnered with Cindy Nazzaro. The moment we met, I knew she was the right person to work with me to build the family-like environment we have. We share in our clients' triumphs, their personal challenges and health issues in their lives as well.

Cindy is in charge of overseeing the team that takes care of our clients with love – something that helps build a different kind of equity long after they start to work with us.

Once you join the Parady Financial Family, you're a member for life.

I may not be able to do that all by myself, but that's where our team comes in. Together, we're able to handle that kind of demand. That's why we only work with people who share our core beliefs and values, and make our homes in the same community as our clients (or nearby outlying areas). We love the fact that we often run into them while we're out and about.

That's what family means.

We also hold regular client appreciation events, and these include an open invitation for people to bring their friends. It's been incredible – our clients have not only grown close to my team and me, but to other clients as well. We've seen friendships forged at our social events that have evolved into dynamic, long-lasting relationships. People who might never have otherwise met are now planning big trips and going on cruises together!

Over the past few years, we've evolved into one huge extended family. When our clients have success, we share in it. When they are hurting, we hurt. We know their kids and their grandchildren, and have celebrated their anniversaries, even in the hospital with those who are recovering from a surgery or other illness. We have a lot of amazing branches in our family tree and when our clients introduce us to their friends who also become clients, that tree continues to grow in wonderful, unanticipated directions. It's a very satisfying way to do business, and to go through life.

I made the decision to switch to this family-style business model in 2007, at the dawn of the financial crisis. The timing made me look like a genius. From 2008-2010, Parady Financial grew exponentially. We tripled in size, going from a relatively successful firm to an extraordinary, producing company in the insurance world. While our family-focused philosophy was certainly a part of that, people also responded positively to how their annuity products and strategies helped provide growth and protection for their retirement assets.

That's because the fun, friendship and family is only the "icing on the cake" of the Parady Financial experience. The cake itself is using insurance products as part of a solid retirement strategy. With our team of CPAs, CFPs and Retirement Planners, we build each family or individual a customized retirement game plan that is intended to last a lifetime.

A huge part of our family success is our Senior VP and CFO Kathie Laseter. Kathie is a veteran CPA and Certified Financial Planner with 25 years of experience. She manages the firm's tax team, including six additional CPAs and accountants. Kathie's diligent, detailed work in the realm of future tax planning is a powerful piece of the overall puzzle of creating successful individual retirement income plans. Kathie has the expertise and experience to help our clients mitigate potential future tax liabilities. Since Parady Financial's focus is on designing strategies that help people get money out of their retirement plans such as IRAs and 401(k)s into more tax-favored, protected products, Kathie's contribution is invaluable. She's a big part of Parady Financial's success.

Because the community of The Villages has been so good to Parady Financial, we do our best to give back. We regularly sponsor fundraisers and work with charities and causes that are important to our team and our clients. These include an annual October breast cancer event, annual food pantry fills, Alzheimer's support groups, Coats for Kids, impromptu Red Cross fundraising, Honor Flight for Veterans, blood drives after natural disasters – and many more. Parady Financial is now also helping fund student lunch programs at several area elementary schools.

We're also keen on the occasional "spontaneous gesture" – the Walmart episode in December 2013 is a prime example. I actually made international news, and earned the nickname "Layaway Santa," for my decision to pay off some customer layaways for 76 families at the local Walmart. We also help fill multiple trailers with goodies for *Toys for Tots* every year.

By being involved in our local community, we keep learning about more ways to help. All of these experiences have inspired me to create the "Parady Cares Foundation," whose initial mission is to address the basic needs of children and the community around The Villages, Florida and in Durango, Colorado, where my family lives part of the year, and where Parady Financial Group has a growing office. It's incredibly rewarding for me, who as a kid, grew up wondering how the bills would get paid and how to support my younger brother and sisters.

CHAPTER 16

BUT ENOUGH ABOUT ME…

Let's talk about you, and your dreams, and your retirement.

How would you feel about retirement funding if you knew exactly how much you were able to spend each month? If you knew exactly how long that money would flow to you? If you knew that even if you live forever, that income would keep coming for the rest of your life.

How would you feel if you had a financial strategy in place that alleviated your concerns about money? How would you feel if your biggest decision was deciding whether your next trip will be a visit to Disney World with the grandchildren, or fulfilling that lifelong dream to visit Australia or Italy, or kicking back and cruising the Caribbean?

How would you feel if you could convert your "bucket list" into a "to-do" list?

My guess is, you would feel pretty good.

But it's not just a guess. My clients live this way every day. And that life has long-term benefits that have nothing to do with money.

Would knowing this change the way you plan things? Would it change your relationship with your spouse, your kids, and your grandkids?

What about the relationship that you have with money?

97

EPILOGUE

FOR MORE INFORMATION

Annuities can provide valuable benefits, with a guaranteed* income being one of the most valuable. We can help you understand how these tools could fit into your retirement strategy, and we can help you look at different products and options for your financial needs and goals. All you have to do is reach out and get the process started.

Thanks for reading and please contact me and my team at **1-800-RETIRED** if you'd like to discuss your retirement goals. You can also check out our website at: www.paradyfinancial.com. In the meantime, I wish you and your family the very best and success in all areas of your life!

By contacting us, you may receive information on the purchase of life insurance and annuity products for purchase.

Multiple References

*Annuity guarantees are backed by the financial strength and claims-paying ability of the issuing carrier.

**Some annuities may have a lifetime income guarantee as part of the base policy; others may have riders available for additional premium that provide this benefit.

SOURCES

1. Udland, Myles. "Long-Term Interest Rates Have Been This Low Only Twice in the Past 214 Years." *BusinessInsider. com*, November 19, 2014. http://www.businessinsider.com/ us-treasury-yields-at-historic-lows-2014-11

2. Fernandes, Deidre. "Health Care Costs Forecast to Rise 7 Percent." *The Boston Globe*, February 5, 2015. http://www.bostonglobe.com/business/2015/02/05/ health-care-costs-rising-driven-drugs-economy/ XYjQjZmbynA5m83bO6PkLJ/story.html

3. "An Interview with Wharton Professor David Babbel - Part One." *Annuity Digest*, date last accessed: March 15, 2015. http://www.annuitydigest.com/blog/tom/interview-wharton-professor-david-babbel-part-one

4. Bureau of Labor Statistics, "Employee Benefits Survey – Table 2, Retirement Benefits: Access, Participation, and Take-Up Rates." March 2012. http://www.bls.gov/ncs/ebs/ benefits/2012/ownership/govt/table02a.

5. Bureau of Labor Statistics, "Employee Benefits Survey Table 3, Retirement benefit combinations: Access, civilianworkers,1 National Compensation Survey." March 2014. http://www.bls.gov/ncs/ebs benefits/2014/ownership/ civilian/table03a.htm

6. Poterba, James, Steven Venti, and David A. Wise. "The Shift from Defined Benefit Pensions to 401(k) Plans and the Pension Assets of the Baby Boom Cohort." Proceedings of the National Academy of Sciences of the United States of America, Vol. 103, No. 33. http://www.pnas.org/content/104/33/13238.full

7. Vernon, Steve. "Pension buyouts: Who Wins and Who Loses?" *MoneyWatch*, October 29, 2012. http://www.cbsnews.com/news/pension-buyouts-who-wins-and-who-loses/

8. *USA Today*, http://usatoday30.usatoday.com/news/washington/2011-06-06-us-debt-chart-medicare-social-security_n.htm

9. Social Security Administration, http://www.ssa.gov/oact/trsum/

10. Research study from the Investment Company Institute, "Frequently Asked Questions about Individual Retirement Accounts (IRAs)." May 2013. http://www.ici.org/faqs/faq/faqs_iras

11. Research study from the A.C. Nielsen Marketing Company, "Introducing Boomers, Marketing's Most Valuable Generation." 2012. http://www.nielsen.com/content/dam/corporate/us/en/reports-downloads/2012-Reports/nielsen-boomers-report-082912.pdf

If you are unable to access any of the articles referenced above, please call 1-800-RETIRED or 352-751-3016 to request a copy.